Fast Cheap Sirtfood Diet Recipes

Little Know Recipes that will Help You Lose Weight Fast while Enjoying Amazing Tastes!

Jorge Krause

SECRET MEALS PUBLISHING

CONTENTS

Salmon & Lentils 5

Salmon with Beans Salad 7

Tofu with Chickpeas & Kale 9

Beans & Veggie Salad 10

Buckwheat Noodles with Beef 11

Buckwheat Noodles with Shrimp 13

Chicken Breast with Asparagus 14
Slow Cooker Salmon & walnut Soup 16
Salmon with Pesto & Beans 17
Mushrooms & Kale Stew 18
Grilled Crunchy Pepper 19
Stir Fried Shrimp & Kale 20
Stir Fry Shrimp & Broccoli 21
Chicken & Veggies Lunch Bowl 22
Lemon Fish Soup 23
Salmon & Potato Soup with Herbs 24
Sweet Corn Soup with Herbs 26
Chicken & Veggies Stew 30
Lentils Soup with Kale 31
Cauliflower & Broccoli Soup 32
Shrimp Soup with Cream 33
Kidney Beans & Tomato Soup 34
Walnut & Chicken Soup 35
Shrimp & Zucchini Stew 36
Beans & Veggies Soup 37
French Lentils Soup 38
Salmon & Beans Soup 39
Instant Pot Salmon Soup 40
Instant Pot Beans Soup 42
Detox Instant Veggies Stew 43
Instant Chicken & Veggies Stew 44
Instant Pot Kale Stew 45
Chicken Snacks 46
Garlic & Cucumber Dip 47
Chocolate Smoothie Jar 48
Beet Root & Kale Hummus 49
Walnut Dip 50
Turmeric & Olives Hummus 50
Chocolate Whipped Cream 51
Creamy Avocado Sauce 52

Healthy Matcha Tea Smoothie 52

Spicy Shrimp Wrap 53

Cardamom Granola Bars 54

Coconut Brownie Bites 56

Kale & Fruit Juice 56

Kale, Carrot, & Grapefruit Juice 58

Buckwheat Granola 59

Apple Pancakes 61

Matcha Pancakes 62

Smoked Salmon & Kale Scramble 64

Kale & Mushroom Frittata 66

Kale, Apple, & Cranberry Salad 68

Arugula, Strawberry, & Orange Salad 69

Beef & Kale Salad 70

Salmon Burgers 72

Chicken with Broccoli & Mushrooms 74

Dijon Celery Salad 117

Cinnamon Apple Chips 121

Potato Bites 122

Beans Snack Salad 123

Sprouts and Apple Snack Salad 124

Salmon & Lentils

Preparation time: 40 Min

Serves: 4

What you need:

For Lentils

- ½ pound French green lentils
- 2 tablespoons extra-virgin olive oil
- 2 cups yellow onions, chopped
- 2 cups scallions, chopped
- 1 teaspoon fresh parsley, chopped
- Salt and ground black pepper, as required
- 1 tablespoon fresh garlic, minced
- 1½ cups carrots, peeled and chopped
- 1½ cups celery stalks, chopped
- 1 tomato, crushed finely
- 1½ cups homemade chicken broth
- 2 tablespoons red wine vinegar

For Salmon

- 4 (6-ounce) skinless salmon fillets
- 2 tablespoons extra-virgin olive oil
- Salt and ground black pepper, as required

Method:

1. In a heat-proof bowl, soak the lentils in boiling water for 15 minutes.

2. Drain the lentils completely.

3. In a Dutch oven, heat the oil over medium heat and cook the onions, scallions, parsley, salt, and black pepper for about **10** minutes, stirring frequently.

4. Add the garlic and cook for about **2** more minutes.

5. Add the drained lentils, carrots, celery, crushed tomato, and broth, and bring to a boil.

6. Reduce the heat to low and simmer, covered for about **20-25** minutes.

7. Stir in the vinegar, salt, and black pepper and remove from the heat.

8. Meanwhile, for salmon: Preheat the oven to 450 degrees F.

9. Rub the salmon fillets with oil and then, season with salt and black pepper generously.

10. Heat an oven-proof sauté pan over medium heat and cook the salmon fillets for about **2** minutes, without stirring.

11. Flip the fillets and immediately transfer the pan into the oven.

12. Bake for about 5-7 minutes or until desired doneness of salmon.

13. Divide the lentil mixture onto serving plates and top each with **1** salmon fillet.

14. Serve hot.

Salmon with Beans Salad

Preparation time: 20 Min

Serves: 4

What you need:

For Salmon

- **2** garlic cloves, minced
- **1** tablespoon fresh lemon zest, grated
- **2** tablespoons extra-virgin olive oil
- **2** tablespoons fresh lemon juice
- Salt and ground black pepper, as required
- 4 (6-ounce) boneless, skinless salmon fillets

For Dressing

- 5 tablespoons fresh orange juice
- 3 tablespoons extra-virgin olive oil
- **1** tablespoon red wine vinegar
- **1** tablespoon honey
- **1** tablespoon fresh orange zest, grated
- ¾ tablespoon Dijon mustard
- Salt and ground black pepper, as required

For Salad

- 3 cups cooked cannellini beans, rinsed and drained
- 6 cups fresh rocket
- **1** cup radishes, quartered
- **1** cup cherry tomatoes, halved
- ½ of red onion, finely sliced
- **2** tablespoons capers, rinsed

Method:

1. Place all salmon Ingredients except for salmon fillets in a bowl and mix well.

2. Add the salmon fillets and coat with garlic mixture generously.

3. Preheat the grill to medium-high heat. Grease the grill grate.

5. Grill the salmon fillets onto the grill and cook for about 6-7 minutes per side.

6. Meanwhile, put all salad ingredients in a bowl and beat until well combined.

7. Mix all dressing ingredients and pour over salad.

8. Divide the beans salad onto serving plates and top each with **1** salmon fillet.

9. Serve immediately.

Tofu with Chickpeas & Kale

Preparation time: 20 Min

Serves: 4

What you need:

For Tofu

- 2 tablespoons extra-virgin olive oil
- 16 ounces tofu, drained, pressed, and cut into 1-inch cubes
- 1 tablespoon low-sodium soy sauce
- 1 teaspoon maple syrup
- 1 teaspoon red pepper flakes, crushed
- ¼ cup filtered water

For Chickpeas & Kale

- 2 tablespoons extra-virgin olive oil
- 3 cups cooked chickpeas, rinsed and drained
- ¼ teaspoon ground turmeric
- Salt and ground black pepper, as required
- 6 cups fresh baby kale
- 1 teaspoon sesame seeds

Method:

1. Heat the olive oil over medium heat and cook the tofu cubes for about 8-10 minutes or until golden from all sides.

2. Add the remaining ingredients and cook for about **2**-3 minutes.

3. Meanwhile, in another sauté pan, heat the oil over medium heat and cook the chickpeas, turmeric, salt, and black pepper for about **2**-3 minutes.

4. Remove the chickpeas from heat and transfer into a large bowl.

5. Add the tofu mixture and kale and stir to combine.

6. Garnish with sesame seeds and serve.

Beans & Veggie Salad

Preparation time: 20 Min

Serves: 4

What you need:

For Dressing

- 4 tablespoons extra-virgin olive oil

- 3 tablespoons fresh lime juice

- **1** tablespoon apple cider vinegar

- **2** tablespoons agave nectar

- Salt & Ground Black Pepper, As Required

For Salad

- 4 cups cooked red kidney beans, rinsed and drained

- **2** cups cherry tomatoes, halved

- **1** cup onion, sliced

- ¼ cup fresh parsley, minced

- 6 cups fresh baby kale

Method:

1. Put all dressing ingredients in a small bowl and beat until well combined.

2. Next, put salad in a bowl, put all ingredients, and mix.

3. Add dressing and toss to coat well.

4. Serve immediately.

Buckwheat Noodles with Beef

Preparation time: 20 Min

Serves: 4

What you need:

For Steak

- **2** tablespoons extra-virgin olive oil

- **1** pound flank steak, sliced thinly

- Salt and ground black pepper, as required

For Salad

- 8 ounces buckwheat noodles

- 4 hard-boiled eggs, peeled and halved

- **1** cup radishes, cut into matchsticks

- **1** cup cucumber, cut into matchsticks

- **1** cup tomato, chopped

- ½ cup scallion greens, chopped

- **1** tablespoon sesame seeds

For Dressing

- ¼ cup fresh orange juice

- 3 tablespoons extra-virgin olive oil

- **2** tablespoons low-sodium soy sauce

- **2** tablespoons white vinegar

- **1** tablespoon fresh lime juice

- **1** tablespoon maple syrup

- **1** teaspoon fresh lime zest, grated

- **1** garlic clove, minced

Method:

1. Heat oil in a large heavy-bottomed pan over medium-high heat and sear the beef slices with salt and black pepper for about 4-5 minutes or until cooked through.

2. Transfer the beef slices onto a plate and set aside.

3. Meanwhile, in a pan of lightly salted boiling water, cook the noodles for about 5 minutes.

4. Drain the noodles well and rinse under cold water.

5. Drain the noodles again.

6. For dressing: Put all ingredients in a bowl and beat until well combined.

7. Divide beef slices, noodles, veggies, and scallion into serving bowls and drizzle with dressing.

8. Garnish with sesame seeds and serve.

Buckwheat Noodles with Shrimp

Preparation time: 20 Min

Serves: 4

What you need:

- 10 ounces buckwheat noodles

- 5 tablespoons extra-virgin olive oil, divided

- 3 tablespoons low-sodium soy sauce

- 3 tablespoons balsamic vinegar

- 1 tablespoon Sriracha

- 1 tablespoon light brown sugar

- 1½ pounds raw shrimp, peeled and deveined

- Salt and ground black pepper, as required

- 1¾ cups zucchini, carrots, julienned

- 1¾ cups carrots, peeled and julienned

Method:

1. Boil noodles in boiling water, cook the noodles for about 5 minutes. Drain and set aside.

2. Meanwhile in a bowl, add 3 tablespoons of oil, soy sauce, vinegar, Sriracha, and brown sugar and beat until well combined. Set aside.

3. Season the shrimp with salt and black pepper lightly.

4. Sautee shrimp in olive oil over medium-high heat and cook the shrimp for about 3-4 minutes, stirring occasionally.

5. Transfer the shrimp onto a plate.

6. In the same skillet, heat the remaining oil over medium-high heat and cook the zucchini and carrots for about 4-5 minutes, stirring occasionally.

7. Remove from heat, and toss with 3 tablespoons of the vinegar mixture.

8. For serving add noodles, shrimp, veggie mixture, and sauce and toss to coat well.

9. Serve immediately

Chicken Breast with Asparagus

Preparation time: 10 Min

Cooking Time 20 min

Total Time 30 Min

Serves: 4

What you need:

For Chicken

- ¼ cup extra-virgin olive oil

- ¼ cup fresh lemon juice

- **2** tablespoons maple syrup

- **1** garlic clove, minced

- Salt and ground black pepper, as required

- 5 (6-ounce) boneless, skinless chicken breasts

For Asparagus

- **1½** pounds fresh asparagus

- **2** tablespoons extra-virgin olive oil

- **1** tablespoon fresh lemon juice

DIRECTION

1. Add oil, lemon juice, Erythritol, garlic, salt, and black pepper in bowl and beat until well combined.

2. Marinate chicken in this mixture for 2 hours.

3. Preheat the grill to medium heat. Grease the grill grate.

4. Remove the chicken from the fridge and discard the marinade.

5. Place the chicken onto grill grate and grill, covered for about 5-8 minutes per side.

6. Place the asparagus in a steamer basket and steam, covered for about 5-7 minutes.

7. Drain the asparagus well and transfer into a bowl.

8. Add oil and lemon juice and toss to coat well.

9. Divide the chicken breasts and asparagus onto serving plates and serve.

Slow Cooker Salmon & walnut Soup

Preparation time: 10 Min

Cooking Time 20 min

Total Time 30 Min

Serves: 4

What you need:

- 1 lb. salmon, cut into cubes
- 1 tbsp. Italian seasoning
- Salt and pepper, to taste
- 1/4 tsp. paprika powder
- 2 tbsps. olive oil
- 1 cup walnut milk
- parsley for topping

Method:

1. Put all ingredients in a slow cooker and cook on low heat for 1 hour.
2. Once cooked remove from the cooker.
3. Drizzle parsley on top.
4. Serve and enjoy!

Salmon with Pesto & Beans

Preparation time: 10 Min

Cooking Time 20 min

Total Time 30 Min

Serves: 2

What you need:

- 2 salmon fillet
- 1 tsp. garlic, minced
- 1 tbsp. Italian seasoning
- Salt and pepper, to taste
- 2 tbsps. olive oil
- green beans for serving
- lemon slice

Pesto sauce

- 1 cup basil leaves
- 1 garlic clove
- tbsp. lime juice
- pinch salt

Method:

1. Toss salmon fillet with garlic, salt, pepper, and Italian seasoning.

2. Heat oil in a pan over medium heat.

3. Add salmon fillet and cook for 4-5 minutes.

4. Flip and cook for another 4-5 minutes until golden brown.

5. Sautee beans along with salmon fillet.

6. Once cooked remove from heat.

7. Meanwhile, blend pesto ingredients in a blender.

8. Drizzle pesto sauce over the salmon fillet.

9. Serve and enjoy!

Mushrooms & Kale Stew

Preparation time: 10 min

Cooking time 30 min

Total time 40 min

Serves: 4

What you need:

- 1/2 lb. mushroom, cut into halves

- 8 oz. kale, chopped

- salt & pepper to taste

- 1 tsp. cumin seeds

- 2 cups. vegetable broth

- 1 tbsp. olive oil

- 2-3 red chili, whole

Method:

1. Heat the oil in a pan over medium heat

2. Once the oil is hot, add mushrooms and cook for 4-5 minutes until mushrooms are reduced.

3. Add kale and cook for 2-3 minutes

4. Season with salt, pepper, and other spices, and add broth and chilies.

5. Cover and cook over medium heat for about 15-20 minutes

6. Once cooked remove from heat.

7. Enjoy.

Grilled Crunchy Pepper

Preparation time: 10 Min

Cooking Time 10 min

Total Time 20 Min

Serves: 4

What you need:

- 1 green bell pepper, cut into thick slice

- 1 red bell pepper, cut into thick slice

- 1 yellow bell pepper, cut into thick slice

- 1 summer squash, sliced

- 1 carrot, peeled and roughly cut

- 1 tbsp. paprika

- Salt and pepper, to taste

- 2 tbsps. olive oil

Method:

1. Season veggies with oil, salt, and pepper.

2. Preheat electric grill over medium heat.

3. Arrange veggies in greased grill grate.

4. Grill veggies for about 5-10 minutes until cooked through.

5. Serve and enjoy!

Stir Fried Shrimp & Kale

Preparation time: 5 Min

Cooking Time 20 min

Total Time 25 Min

Serves: 4

What you need:

- 1 tsp garlic, minced

- 2 cup chopped kale

- 1 onion, chopped

- 1 lb. shrimp, trimmed

- ½ cup chopped tomatoes

- salt and pepper to taste

- 1 tbsp. olive oil

- 1 tbsps. lime juice

Method:

1. Heat the oil in a pan over medium heat.

2. Once the oil is hot, add onion and garlic and cook for 2-3 minutes.

3. Add spinach in the same pan and cook for 5-6 minutes until kale is welted.

4. Add tomatoes and just cook for 2-3 minutes more.

5. Add shrimp and cook for 4-5 minutes until veggies are dried.

6. Once cooked remove from heat.

7. Drizzle lime juice on top.

8. Serve and enjoy!

Stir Fry Shrimp & Broccoli

Preparation time: 5 Min

Cooking Time 15min

Total Time 20 Min

Serves: 8

What you need:

- 1 broccoli head, cut into florets

- 1 cauliflower head, florets

- 2-3 carrots, sliced

- baby corn sliced

- lb. peeled and deveined shrimp

- 1 tbsp. extra virgin olive oil

- lemon juice

- 1 tsp. fresh chopped dill

- 1 tbsp. fresh chopped oregano

- ½ tsp smoked paprika

- ½ tsp sea salt

- ¼ tsp black pepper

Method:

1. Heat your large frying pan over high heat, add oil.

2. Once the oil is hot, vegetables and fries for about 5-8 minutes.

3. Add dill, oregano, paprika, salt, and pepper, and mix well.

4. Add shrimp and cook covered for 5-8 minutes until all veggies are cooked through.

5. Once cooked remove from heat.

6. Drizzle lemon juice on top.

7. Serve and enjoy.

Chicken & Veggies Lunch Bowl

Preparation time: 5 Min

Cooking Time 15 min

Total Time 20 Min

Serves: 4

What you need:

- 1 chicken breast

- 1 tbsp. extra-virgin olive oil

- 1 red onion, finely sliced

- 4-5 fresh tomatoes, sliced

- kale leaves, chopped

- 1 lime juice

- salt & pepper to taste

Method:

1. Coat chicken breast with oil, salt, and pepper all over. Grill chicken breast in a grill for about 5-10 minutes until cooked and brown.

2. Once cooked remove the breast from the grill.

3. Cut breast in bite-size pieces.

4. Assemble chopped kale leaves and tomato slices in a bowl.

5. Top with chicken breast.

6. Drizzle lime juice, salt, and pepper on top.

7. Serve and enjoy!

Lemon Fish Soup

Preparation time: 10 Min

Cooking Time 20 min

Total Time 30 Min

Serves: 4

What you need:

- 10 cups chicken broth
- 3 tbsps. olive oil
- 1 onion, chopped
- 1 large lemon, zested
- 2 salmon fillets in halves
- Salt and pepper
- ¼ cup green onion

Method:

1. Heat the oil in a large pan over medium heat.
2. Add onion and cook for 2-3 minutes.
3. Add salmon cubes and cook for 4-5 minutes until cooked through.
4. Add chicken broth and season with salt, and pepper.
5. Bring broth to boil and simmer on low flame for about 20-25 minutes until chicken is cooked.
6. Sprinkle green onion and lime juice on top.
7. Serve immediately.
8. Enjoy!

Salmon & Potato Soup with Herbs

Preparation time: 5 Min

Cooking time 40 Min

Total time 45 Min

Serves: 6

What you need:

- 1 lb. salmon fillet cut into cubes
- 2-3 medium potatoes, cut into
- 2 tbsps. extra virgin olive oil
- 1 tbsp. onion powder.
- 1 tbsps. garlic powder
- 1/4 tsp. black pepper
- 1/2 tsp. salt
- warm water to cover
- 1 tbsp. lime juice

Method:

1. Heat large heavy pot over medium heat, add oil.
2. Once the oil is hot, add salmon cubes and cook for about 4-5 minutes until cooked and no pinker.
3. Add tomatoes and cook for again 4-5 minutes.
4. Add onion, garlic powder, salt, and pepper in the same pot and mix well.
5. Add 6 cups of hot water to cover completely.
6. Cook covered for about 30 minutes to simmer on low heat.
7. Once cooked remove from heat.

8. Serve hot and enjoy!

Sweet Corn Soup with Herbs

Preparation time: 5 Min

Cooking time 20 Min

Total time 25 Min

Serves: 4

What you need:

- 2 tbsp. olive oil

- 1 tsp. garlic, minced

- 1 can sweet corns, drained

- 6 cups chicken stock

- Salt to taste

- Pepper to taste

- 1 tbsp. lime juice

- Parsley

Method:

1. Heat the oil in a large pot over medium heat.

2. Once the oil is hot, add garlic and sauté for about 1 minute.

3. Add sweet corns, broth and cook for about 3-4 minutes.

4. Season with salt and pepper and mix well.

5. Cover and cook on low heat for about 15 minutes.

6. Pour soup in a blender and blend for 5 -10 seconds.

7. Pour soup into a serving bowl.

8. Top with some sweet corns and parsley and lime juice.

9. Enjoy!

Traditional Russian Cold Soup

Preparation time: 10 Min

Cooking Time 20 Min

Total Time 30 Min

Serves: 4

What you need:

- 1 boil potato, chopped
- ¼ cup tomatoes, chopped
- 2 cups walnut cream
- 1 red onion, chopped
- 1 cucumber, chopped
- 1 oz. rosemary, chopped
- ⅛ tsp black pepper
- ¼ tsp salt
- 2 tbsps. olive oil

Method:

1. Mix potato, tomato, onion, cucumber, and rosemary in a bowl.
2. Add walnut cream and mix well.
3. Season with salt and pepper, and mix well.
4. Drizzle olive oil on top.
5. Serve and enjoy!

Chicken Soup with Carrots

Preparation time: 5 Min

Cooking Time 25 Min

Total Time 30 Min

Serves: 4

What you need:

- 1 chicken breast,
- 1 carrot, sliced
- 1 tbsp. olive oil
- 1 tsp garlic, minced
- 4 cups chicken broth
- Salt and pepper to taste
- ¼ cup parsley leaves

Method:

1. Heat the oil in a 10-inch skillet, once the oil is hot, add chicken and garlic and cook for 3-4 minutes, until the chicken is no longer pink.
2. Season with salt, pepper, and mix well.
3. Add carrot and broth.
4. Cover and cook on low heat for 25-30 minutes until veggies are cooked.
5. Slightly shredded chicken with hand or spatula.
6. Sprinkle parsley leaves on top.

7. Serve and enjoy hot.

Chicken & Veggies Stew

Preparation time: 10 Min

Cooking Time 20 Min

Total time 30 Min

Serves: 4

What you need:

- 1 tbsp. olive oil
- 1/2 lb. chicken, boil and shredded
- 1 carrot, sliced
- ¼ cup green peas
- 4 cups chicken stock
- 1/2 tsp salt
- 1/4 tsp black pepper
- 1 tbsp. lime juice.
- 1/4 cup chopped parsley

Method:

1. Heat the olive oil in a non-stick soup pot over medium heat.

2. Once the oil is hot, add chicken, carrots, peas, and sauté for about 4-5 minutes.

3. Add the stock and season with salt, and pepper.

4. Cook covered for about 15-20 minutes on low heat until veggies are cooked through

5. Sprinkle lime juice on top.

6. Adjust seasoning according to taste and enjoy!

Lentils Soup with Kale

Preparation time: 10 Min

Cooking time 20 Min

Total time 40 Min

Serves: 4

What you need:

- 2 tbsps. olive oil
- 1 red onion, chopped
- 1/4 cup red lentils, soaked and drained
- 4 cups chicken broth
- salt & pepper to taste
- 2 cups kale

Topping

- 1 tomato, chopped
- 1 onion chopped
- Parsley
- 1 tbsps. lime juice

Method:

1. Heat the oil in a saucepan over medium heat.

2. Once the oil is hot, add onion and cook for about 2-3 minutes.

3. Add lentils, broth, kale and cook covered for about 15-20 minutes.

4. Season with salt to taste mix well.

5. Add tomatoes, onion, parsley, and lime juice and mix well.

6. Serve and enjoy!

Cauliflower & Broccoli Soup

Preparation time: 15 Min

Cooking Time 20 Min

Total Time 35 Min

Serves: 4

What you need:

- 1 medium broccoli florets

- 1 medium, cauliflower

- 1 tsp garlic, minced

- 1 tbsp. olive oil

- 4 cups chicken stock

- 1 tsp salt

- 1 tsp pepper

- 1 pinch curry powder

- 1 tbsp. parsley chopped

- 1 white onion, sliced

Method:

1. Heat the oil in a pan over medium heat.

2. Once the oil is hot, cook broccoli and cauliflower with garlic for about 4-5 minutes.

3. Add broth and simmer on low to medium heat for 15-20 minutes.

4. Add in salt, pepper, curry powder, onion slice, and parsley.

5. Adjust seasoning to taste.

6. Serve hot and enjoy!

Shrimp Soup with Cream

Preparation time: 05 Min

Cooking time 20 Min

Total time 25 Min

Serves: 4

What you need:

- 1 tbsp. olive oil

- 1 lb. shrimp,

- 2 cups kale chopped

- 1 tomato sliced

- 4 cups chicken stock

- 1 tsp. curry powder

- 1 cup walnut cream

- salt and pepper, to taste

- pinch of chili powder

Method:

1. Heat the olive oil in a saucepan over medium heat.

2. Once the oil is hot, add shrimp and cook for another 2-3 minutes.

3. Season with salt, pepper, curry powder, chili powder, and add kale.

4. Add in cream, chicken stock, and mix well.

5. Cover and simmer for about 5-8 minutes on low heat.

6. Pour soup in a soup bowl with a tomato slice.

7. Drizzle lime juice on top.

8. Serve hot.

Kidney Beans & Tomato Soup

Preparation time: 10 Min

Cooking time 30 Min

Total time 40 Min

Serves: 4

What you need:

- 2 tbsps. olive oil

- 1 can kidney beans, drained
- 1 cup tomato puree
- 1 cup tomato chopped
- 3 small onion rings
- 6 cups chicken stock
- salt and pepper to taste

Method:

1. Place kidney beans, onion rings,

stock, and tomato puree in a large stockpot over medium heat.

2. Bring to a simmer, cover, and cook for about 20 minutes, until the soup is thick.

3. Add salt, pepper and mix well.

4. Taste and add salt, if needed.

5. Add chopped tomatoes and serve.

6. Enjoy hot!

Walnut & Chicken Soup

Preparation time:: 5 min

Cooking Time 25 min

Total Time 30 min

Serves: 4

Ingredients

- 1 chicken breast, cut into cubes

- 1/2 lb. button mushrooms. sliced

- 1 cup walnut cream

- salt and pepper, to taste

- 6 cups. chicken stock

- 4-5 whole red pepper

- parsley

Method:

1. Heat the oil in a pan, once the oil is hot, add chicken, cook for about 5-8 minutes until the chicken is no longer pink.

2. Add stock, red pepper, cream, and cook covered for about 8-10 minutes.

3. Season with salt and pepper and mix well.

4. Pour soup in bowls.

5. Serve and enjoy!

Shrimp & Zucchini Stew

Preparation time: 5 Min

Cooking time 15 Min

Total time 20 Min

Serves: 4

What you need:

- 1 tbsp. olive oil

- 1 lb. shrimp, peeled

- 1 zucchini, roughly sliced
- 1 bunch kale, trimmed and chopped
- ¼ cup chopped onion
- ½ tsp. salt and pepper
- 4 cups chicken broth

Method:.

1. Heat the oil in a large pot over

medium heat.

2. Once the oil is hot, add onion and sauté for about 2-3 minutes until onions are transparent.
3. Stir in the shrimp, zucchini, kale, chicken broth and season with salt and pepper.
4. Bring boil to a simmer for about 5-8 minutes until shrimp and veggies are cooked.
5. Sprinkle parsley leaves on top.
6. Enjoy!

Beans & Veggies Soup

Preparation time: 5 Min

Cooking Time 25 Min

Total Time 30 Min

Serves: 4

What you need:

- 2 cups chopped broccoli

- 1 cup kale, chopped
- 1 cup kidney beans, drained
- 2 tbsps. onion powder
- 3 cups chicken stock
- 1 tbsp. olive oil
- 1/4 tsp. salt
- 1/8 tsp. pepper
- 1 tbsp. lime juice

Method:

1. Heat oil in pan over medium heat.
2. Once oil is hot, add broccoli and carrot, cook for about 3-5 minutes, until veggies turn into brown.
3. Add stock, beans, kale, salt, pepper in pan and mix well.
4. Cover and cook on low heat for about 10-12 minutes until veggies are cooked through.
5. Drizzle lime juice on top.
6. Serve hot and enjoy!

French Lentils Soup

Preparation time: 10 Min

Cooking Time: 20 Min

Total Time: 30 Min

Serves: 4

Ingredients

- 1 tbsp. olive oil
- 1 cup French lentils, soaked and drained
- Salt and pepper
- 1 tsp. garlic, minced
- 1 onion chopped
- 6 cups chicken broth
- salt and pepper to taste
- 1 tomato, chopped
- parsley chopped

Method:

1. In a large saucepan over medium heat, heat the oil.
2. Sautee onion and garlic for about 3-4 minutes.
3. Add lentils, broth and bring to a boil, simmer for about 30-35 minutes until lentils are tendered.
4. Season with salt and pepper and mix well.
5. Top with tomato and parsley.
6. Drizzle lime juice on top.
7. Serve and enjoy!

Salmon & Beans Soup

Preparation time:: 10 Min

Cooking Time: 25 Min

Total Time: 35 Min

Serves: 4

Ingredients

- 1 tbsp. olive oil
- 8 oz. green beans
- 1 carrot, chopped
- 1 salmon slice, cut into slice
- 1 garlic clove, minced
- 4 cups chicken stock
- 1/2 tsp salt
- 1/4 tsp black pepper

Method:

1. Heat the oil in a nonstick soup pot, add salmon and cook with garlic for about 4-5 minutes.
2. Add the stock, beans, carrots, seasoning, and bring to boil, simmer for about 15 minutes.
3. Drizzle parsley lemon juice and mix well.
4. Serve and enjoy

Instant Pot Salmon Soup

Preparation time: 5 Min

Cooking Time 20 Min

Total Time 25 Min

Serves: 4

What you need:

- 1 salmon fillet cut into cubes
- 1/2 cup onion, chopped
- 1 bunch kale, chopped
- 1 tsp. garlic, minced
- 1 tsp. cumin seed powder
- ½ tsp. sea salt
- 2 tbsps. lemon juice
- 4 cups chicken broth

Topping

- 8 oz. walnut cream
- 1 oz. rosemary, chopped

Method:

1. Put all ingredients into an Instant Pot.
2. Cover, close the lid, and cook on high pressure for about 18 minutes.
3. Allow pressure to release naturally, about 10 minutes, before removing the lid.
4. Add the rosemary and cream on top and stir well.
5. Serve immediately.

Instant Pot Beans Soup

Preparation time: 5 Min

Cooking Time 20 Min

Total Time 25 Min

Serves: 4

What you need:

- 1 cup kidney beans, boil
- 1 cup white beans, cooked
- 1 bunch kale, chopped
- 1 cup green onion, chopped
- 1 tsp. garlic, minced
- 1 tsp. cumin seed powder
- ½ tsp. sea salt
- 2 tbsps. olive oil
- 2 tbsps. lemon juice
- 4 cups water

Method:

1. Put all ingredients with broth in an Instant Pot.
2. Cover, close the lid, and cook on high pressure for about 18 minutes.
3. Allow pressure to release naturally, about 10 minutes, before removing the lid.

4. Serve immediately.

5. Enjoy!

Detox Instant Veggies Stew

Preparation time: 5 Min

Cooking time 5 Min

Total time 10 Min

Serves: 1

What you need:

- 1 carrot, sliced

- 8 oz. green beans

- 2 cups broccoli, florets

- 1 cup cauliflower, florets.

- 1 zucchini, sliced

- 1 cup green onion, chopped

- 1 tsp. garlic, minced

- 1 tbsp. curry powder

- 1 tsp. cumin seed powder

- ½ tsp. sea salt

- 2 tbsps. olive oil

- 2 tbsps. lemon juice

- 4 cups water

Method:

1. Put all ingredients with broth in an Instant Pot.

2. Cover, close the lid, and cook on high pressure for about 18 minutes.

3. Allow pressure to release naturally, about 10 minutes, before removing the lid.

4. Serve immediately.

5. Enjoy!

Instant Chicken & Veggies Stew

Preparation time: 10 Min

Cooking Time 20 Min

Total Time 30 Min

Serves: 6

What you need:

- 2 tbsps. garlic, minced

- 3 cups chicken broth

- 1 lb. mushrooms, halves

- 2 cups coconut cream

- 1 cup broccoli, florets

- ⅛ tsp white pepper

- ¼ tsp salt

- 2 tbsps. olive oil

- 1 green onion, sliced

- 4-5 cherry tomatoes

Method:

1. Heat the oil in a pan over medium heat, add garlic and mushrooms and broccoli, cook until mushrooms and broccoli are brown and shrink.

2. Add chicken broth, cream salt, and pepper and cook for another 5-6 minutes over medium heat.

3. Once soup is cooked remove from heat.

4. Sprinkle green onion on top.

5. Enjoy!

Instant Pot Kale Stew

Preparation time: 10 min

Cooking time 20 min

Total time 30 min

Serves: 4

What you need:

- 1 onion, chopped

- 1 bunch kale, chopped \

- 2 cup cauliflower, roughly chopped

- 1 cup potato, chopped

- 1 cup green peas.

- 1 tsp garlic, minced

- 4 cups vegetable broth

- 2 tbsps. olive oil

- Salt, black pepper to taste

- 2 lime juice

- 1/2 cup parsley, chopped

Method:

1. Put all ingredients with broth in an Instant Pot.

2. Cover, close the lid, and cook on high pressure for about 18 minutes.

3. Allow pressure to release naturally, about 10 minutes, before removing the lid.

4. Add chopped parsley on top and stir well.

5. Serve immediately.

Chicken Snacks

Preparation time: 15 Min

Cooking Time 10 min

Total Time 25 Min

Serves: 4

What you need:

- 2 chicken breast, ground

- 1/2 cup buckwheat flour

- 2 tbsps. onion powder

- 2 tbsps. garlic powder

- 1 tsp. dried oregano

- 1 tsp. paprika powder

- 1 tsp. salt

- 1/2 tsp. black pepper

- 2 tbsps. olive oil

Method:

1. Mix flour, onion, garlic powder, oregano, paprika powder, salt, black pepper, and chicken in a bowl and set aside.

2. Make oval kebab by this mixture,

3. Heat the oil in a 10-inch skillet, add oil.

4. Once the oil is hot, place the chicken kebab in skillet and cook for 6-8 minutes.

5. Serve with BBQ sauce and enjoy.

Garlic & Cucumber Dip

Preparation time:: 10 min

Serves: 4

What you need:

- 1 cucumber, chopped

- 1 tsp. garlic, minced

- 1 tbsp. chopped shallot

- 2 tsps. olive oil

- 1/2 tsp. Italian seasoning

- 1/8 tsp. salt

- 1 cup mint leaves

- I cup walnut cream

Method:

1. Put all ingredients in a food processor except cream and blend until mixed.

2. Mix this paste with cream in a mixing bowl.

3. Adjust salt according to taste.

4. Serve and enjoy!

Chocolate Smoothie Jar

Preparation time: 10 min

Serves: 2

What you need:

- 1 cup walnut milk

- ¼ cup cocoa powder

- 2 tbsps. chia seeds

- TOPPING

- Strawberries

Method:

1. Mix milk, chia seeds, and cocoa powder in a bowl and leave overnight in the fridge.

2. In the morning top smoothie with strawberries slice.

3. Serve and enjoy!

Beet Root & Kale Hummus

Preparation time:: 10 min

Serves: 4

What you need:

- 1/4 cup walnut butter
- 1/4 cup lemon juice
- 1 tbsp. olive oil
- 1 cup kale chopped
- 1 cup beetroot, chopped
- 1/4 tsp. sea salt
- 1/4 tsp. cayenne pepper
- 1/4 tsp. ground turmeric
- 1 tbsp. parsley, chopped

Method:

1. Put all ingredients in a food processor and blend until mixed. Once mixed, pour in a bowl.

2. Adjust salt according to taste.

3. Drizzle olive oil, chickpeas and sesame seeds on top

4. Serve and enjoy!

Walnut Dip

Preparation time:: 5 min

Serves: 4

What you need:

- 1/4 cup walnuts, sacked whole night
- 4 cloves garlic, chopped
- 2 tbsps. fresh lemon juice
- 1 tbsp. olive oil
- ¾ cup water
- 2 tbsps. fresh parsley leaves salt and pepper to taste

Method:

1. Put all ingredients in a blender and blend.
1. Process until a paste is smooth and fluffy.
2. Season with salt and pepper and mix well.
3. Serve with chicken nuggets.

Turmeric & Olives Hummus

Preparation time: 10 Min

Serves: 8

What you need:

- 1/4 cup tahini
- 1/4 cup lemon juice
- 1 tbsp. olive oil

- 1/2 cup capers

- 1 tbsp. nutritional yeast

- 1/4 tsp. sea salt

- 1/4 tsp. cayenne pepper

- 1/4 tsp. ground turmeric

- 1 tbsp. parsley, chopped

Method:

1. Put all ingredients in a high-speed food processor and mix thoroughly.

2. If the dressing seems too thick, add a little more water.

3. Top with cayenne and chopped parsley.

4. Serve and enjoy!

Chocolate Whipped Cream

Preparation time: 10 Min

Serves: 10

What you need:

- 3 cups coconut cream cold

- 1/2 cup cocoa powder

- 1/2 cup coconut sugar

Method:

1. Beat cream with blender, add sugar and cocoa powder, and beat again for 5-10 minutes.

2. Serve on ice cream or toast.

Creamy Avocado Sauce

Preparation time: 10 Min

Serves: 10

What you need:

- 3 cups walnut cream cold

- 1 lime juice

- 1 tsp. garlic, mashed

- 2 avocados mashed

Method:

1. Beat cream with blender and beat for 5-10 minutes.

2. Add the rest of the ingredients and beat again.

3. Serve on ice cream or toast.

Healthy Matcha Tea Smoothie

Preparation time: 10 min

Serves: 2

What you need:

- 1/2 cup walnut cream

- 1 cup avocado chopped

- 1 cup mint leaves

- 1 tbsp. matcha green tea powder

Topping

- 1 kiwi fruit, sliced
- 2 oz. blueberries
- 2 oz. raspberries
- 1 oz. chopped nuts
- 1 oz. pumpkin seeds

Method:

1. Add cream, avocado, mint, and green tea powder in an electric blender.

2. Blend well until creamy and smooth.

3. Top with kiwi slice, blueberries, raspberries, nuts, and pumpkin seeds.

4. Serve and enjoy!

Spicy Shrimp Wrap

Preparation time:: 5 min

Cooking Time: 20 min

Total Time: 25 min

Serves: 4

What you need:

- 4 buckwheat tortillas
- 1 lb. shrimp, peeled
- 5-8 cherry tomatoes, cut into two
- 1/2 tsp Italian seasoning

- 1 avocado, chopped
- ½ cup green peas
- 1 tbsp. olive oil
- arugula leaves
- 1 lemon, sliced

Method:

1. Heat the oil in a pan over medium heat.
2. Once the oil is hot, add shrimp and cook for 4-5 minutes until cooked.
3. Season with Italian seasoning and mix well.
4. Once cooked remove from heat.
5. Toss the tortilla on a griddle for 2-3 minutes.
6. Lay the tortilla on a plate.
7. Spread arugula leaves on each tortilla.
8. Divide shrimp, avocado, tomatoes, and peas on each tortilla.
9. Drizzle lime juice, paprika on each tortilla and serve!

Cardamom Granola Bars

Preparation time: **5 minutes**

Cooking time: **30 minutes**

Servings: **3**

What you need:

- 2 cups rolled oats
- ½ cup raisins
- ½ cup walnuts, chopped and toasted
- 1 ½ teaspoons ground cardamom
- 6 tablespoons cocoa butter
- 1/3 cup packed brown sugar
- 3 tablespoons honey
- Coconut oil, for greasing pan

Method:

1. Preheat oven to 350 degrees F.

2. Line a 9-inch square pan with foil, extending the foil over the sides. Grease the foil with coconut oil.

3. Mix the oats, raisins, walnuts and cardamom in a large bowl.

4. Heat the cocoa butter, brown sugar and honey in a saucepan until the butter melts and begins to bubble.

5. Bake for 30 minutes or until the top is golden brown.

6. Allow to cool for 30 minutes. Using the foil, lift the granola out of the pan and place on cutting board.

7. Cut into 18 bars.

Per serving:

Calories 232, fat 5.5, fiber 7.5, carbs 20.9, protein 16.8

Coconut Brownie Bites

Preparation time: **5 minutes**

Cooking time: **40 minutes**

Servings: **3**

What you need:

- ¼ cup unsweetened cocoa powder

- ¼ cup unsweetened desiccated or shredded coconut

Method:

1. Place everything in a food processor and blend until well combined.

2. Roll into 1" balls.

3. Roll balls in coconut until well-covered and place on wax paper lined baking sheet.

4. Freeze for 30 minutes or refrigerate for up to 2 hours.

Per serving:

Calories 282, fat 11.5, fiber 5.5, carbs 17.9, protein 14.8

Kale & Fruit Juice

Preparation Time: **10 minutes**

Cooking Time: **10 minutes**

Servings: **2**

What you need:

- 2 large green apples, cored and sliced

- Large pears, cored and sliced

- 3 cups fresh kale leaves

- 3 celery stalks

- 1 lemon, peeled

Method:

1. Add all **ingredients** into a juicer

2. and extract the juice according to the manufacturer's method.

3. Pour into 2 glasses and serve immediately.

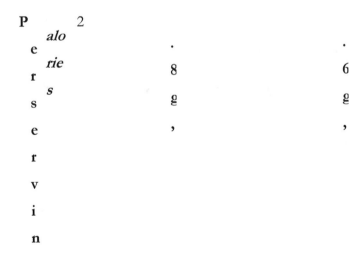

P   2
  alo
 e
  rie   .   .
 r
            8   6
  s
 s   g   g
 e   ,   ,
 r
 v
 i
 n

Kale, Carrot, & Grapefruit Juice

Preparation Time: **10 minutes**

Cooking Time: **10 minutes**

Servings: **2**

What you need:

- 3 cups fresh kale

- 2 large Granny Smith apples, cored and sliced

- 2 medium carrots, peeled and chopped

- 2 medium grapefruit, peeled

- 1 teaspoon fresh lemon juice

Method:

1. Add all **ingredients** into a juicer.

2. and extract the juice according to the manufacturer's method.

3. Pour into 2 glasses and serve immediately.

C   5

0   7   4

.   .   .

6   7   9

g   g   g

,   ,   ,

Buckwheat Granola

Preparation Time: **15 minutes**

Cooking Time: **30 minutes**

Servings: **10**

What you need:

- 2 cups raw buckwheat groats

- ¾ cup pumpkin seeds

- ¾ cup almonds, chopped

- 1 cup unsweetened coconut flakes

- 1 teaspoon ground cinnamon

- 1 teaspoon ground ginger

- 1 ripe banana, peeled

- 2 tablespoons maple syrup

- 2 tablespoons olive oil

Method:

1. Preheat your oven to 350°F. In a bowl, place the buckwheat groats, coconut flakes, pumpkin seeds, almonds and spices and mix well.

2. In another bowl, add the banana and with a fork, mash well.

3. Add to the buckwheat mixture maple syrup and oil and mix until well combined.

4. Transfer the mixture onto the prepared baking sheet and spread in an even layer. Bake for about 25–30 minutes, stirring once halfway through.

5. Remove the baking sheet from oven and set aside to cool.

		S
		o
4.	7.	d
3	6	i
g,	g,	u
		n

Apple Pancakes

Preparation Time: **15 minutes**

Cooking Time: **24 minutes**

Servings: **6**

What you need:

- ½ cup buckwheat flour
- 2 tablespoons coconut sugar
- 1 teaspoon baking powder
- ½ teaspoon ground cinnamon
- 1/3 cup unsweetened almond milk
- 1 egg, beaten lightly
- 2 granny smith apples, peeled, coredand grated

Method:

1. In a bowl, place the flour, coconut sugarand cinnamonand mix well.

2. In another bowl, place the almond milk and egg and beat until well combined.

3. Now, place the flour mixture and mix until well combined.

4. Fold in the grated apples.

5. Heat a lightly greased non-stick wok over medium-high heat.

6. Add desired amount of mixture and with a spoon, spread into an even layer.

7. Cook for 1–2 minutes on each side.

8. Repeat with the remaining mixture.

9. Serve warm with the drizzling of honey.

.1 g, .5 g,

S
o
d
i
u
m

Matcha Pancakes

Preparation Time: **15 minutes**

Cooking Time: **24 minutes**

Servings: 6

What you need:

- 2 tablespoons flax meal

- 5 tablespoons warm water

- 1 cup spelt flour

- 1 cup buckwheat flour

- 1 tablespoon matcha powder

- 1 tablespoon baking powder

- Pinch of salt

- ¾ cup unsweetened almond milk

- 1 tablespoon olive oil

- 1/3 cup raw honey

Method:

1. In a bowl, add the flax meal and warm water and mix well. Set aside for about 5 minutes.

2. In another bowl, place the flours, matcha powder, baking powder and salt and mix well.

3. In the bowl of flax meal mixture, place the almond milk, oil and vanilla extract and beat until well combined.

4. Now, place the flour mixture and mix until a smooth textured mixture is formed.

5. Heat a lightly greased non-stick wok over medium-high heat.

6. Add desired amount of mixture and with a spoon, spread into an even layer.

7. Cook for about 2–3 minutes.

8. Carefully, flip the side and cook for about 1 minute.

9. Repeat with the remaining mixture.

10. Serve warm with the drizzling of honey.

Smoked Salmon & Kale Scramble

Preparation Time: **10 minutes**

Cooking Time: **9 minutes**

Servings: 3

What you need:

- 2 cups fresh kale, tough ribs removed and chopped finely

- 1 tablespoon coconut oil

- Ground black pepper, to taste

- ½ cup smoked salmon, crumbled

- 4 eggs, beaten

Method:

1. In a wok, melt the coconut oil over high heat and cook the kale with black pepper for about 3–4 minutes.

2. Stir in the smoked salmon and reduce the heat to medium.

3. Add the eggs and cook for about 3–4 minutes, stirring frequently.

4. Serve immediately.

Kale & Mushroom Frittata

Preparation Time: **15 minutes**

Cooking Time: **30 minutes**

Servings: 5

What you need:

- 8 eggs
- ½ cup unsweetened almond milk
- Salt and ground black pepper, to taste
- 1 tablespoon olive oil
- 1 onion, chopped
- 1 garlic clove, minced
- 1 cup fresh mushrooms, chopped
- 1½ cups fresh kale, tough ribs removed and chopped

Method:

1. Preheat oven to 350°F.
2. In a large bowl, place the eggs, coconut milk, salt and black pepper.
3. and beat well. Set aside.

4. In a large ovenproof wok, heat the oil over medium heat.

5. and sauté the onion and garlic for about 3–4 minutes.

6. Add the squash, kale, bell pepper, salt and black pepper.

7. and cook for about 8–10 minutes.

8. Stir in the mushrooms and cook for about 3–4 minutes.

9. Add the kale and cook for about 5 minutes.

10. Place the egg mixture on top evenly.

11. and cook for about 4 minutes, without stirring.

12. Transfer the wok in the oven.

13. and bake for about 12–15 minutes or until desired doneness.

14. Remove from the oven.

15. and place the frittata side for about 3–5 minutes before serving.

16. Cut into desired sized wedges and serve.

1	1
0	0
.	.
2	3
g	g
,	,

Kale, Apple, & Cranberry Salad

Preparation Time: **15 minutes**

Cooking Time: **15 minutes**

Servings: 4

What you need:

- 6 cups fresh baby kale

- 3 large apples, cored and sliced

- ¼ cup unsweetened dried cranberries

- ¼ cup almonds, sliced

- 2 tablespoons extra-virgin olive oil

- 1 tablespoon raw honey

- Salt and ground black pepper, to taste

Method:

1. In a salad bowl, place all the ingredients and toss to coat well.

2. Serve immediately.

Per serving: Calories 53, Fat 10.3g, Carbs 40.7g, Protein 4.7g, Sodium 84mg

Arugula, Strawberry, & Orange Salad

Preparation Time: **15 minutes**

Cooking Time: **15 minutes**

Servings: 4

What you need:

- Salad

- 6 cups fresh baby arugula

- 1½ cups fresh strawberries, hulled and sliced

- 2 oranges, peeled and segmented

- Dressing

- 2 tablespoons fresh lemon juice

- 1 tablespoon raw honey

- 2 teaspoons extra-virgin olive oil

- 1 teaspoon Dijon mustard

- Salt and ground black pepper, to taste

Method:

1. For salad: in a salad bowl, place all **ingredients** and mix.

2. For dressing: place all **ingredients** in another bowl and beat until well combined.

3. Place dressing on top of salad and toss to coat well.

4. Serve immediately.

C

Beef & Kale Salad

Preparation Time: **15 minutes**

Cooking Time: **8 minutes**

Servings: **2**

What you need:

- For Steak

- 2 teaspoons olive oil

- 2 (4-ounce) strip steaks

- Salt and ground black pepper, to taste

- Salad

- ¼ cup carrot, peeled and shredded

- ¼ cup cucumber, peeled, seededand sliced

- ¼ cup radish, sliced

- ¼ cup cherry tomatoes, halved

- 3 cups fresh kale, tough ribs removed and chopped

- For Dressing

- 1 tablespoon extra-virgin olive oil

- 1 tablespoon fresh lemon juice

- Salt and ground black pepper, to taste

Method:

1. For steak: in a large heavy-bottomed wok.

2. Heat the oil over high heat.

3. Cook the steaks with salt and black pepper for about 3–4 minutes per side.

4. Transfer the steaks onto a cutting board for about 5 minutes before slicing.

5. For salad: place all **ingredients** in a salad bowl and mix.

6. For dressing: place all **ingredients** in another bowl and beat until well combined.

7. Cut the steaks into desired sized slices against the grain.

8. Place the salad onto each serving plate.

9. Top each plate with steak slices.

10. Drizzle with dressing and serve.

Per serving: **Calories** 262, **] 12 g, at** **Carbs** 15.2g **Protein** 25.2g **Sodium** 506mg

Salmon Burgers

Preparation Time: **20 minutes**

Cooking Time: **15 minutes**

Servings: **5**

What you need:

- For Burgers
- 1 teaspoon olive oil
- 1 cup fresh kale, tough ribs removed and chopped
- 1/3 cup shallots, chopped finely
- Salt and ground black pepper, to taste
- 16 ounces skinless salmon fillets
- ¾ cup cooked quinoa

- 2 tablespoons Dijon mustard

- 1 large egg, beaten

- For Salad

- 2½ tablespoons olive oil

- 2½ tablespoons red wine vinegar

- Salt and ground black pepper, to taste

- 8 cups fresh baby arugula

- 2 cups cherry tomatoes, halved

Method:

1. **For burgers: in a large non-stick wok, heat the oil over medium heat and sauté the kale, shallots, salt and black pepper for about 4–5 minutes.**

2. Remove from heat and transfer the kale mixture into a large bowl.

3. Set aside to cool slightly.

4. With a knife, chop 4 ounces of salmon and transfer into the bowl of kale mixture.

5. In a food processor, add the remaining salmon and pulse until finely chopped.

6. Transfer the finely chopped salmon into the bowl of kale mixture.

7. Then, add remaining **ingredients** and stir until fully combined.

8. Make 5 equal-sized patties from the mixture.

9. Heat a lightly greased large non-stick wok over medium heat and cook the patties for about 4–5 minutes per side.

10. For dressing: in a glass bowl, add the oil, vinegar, shallots, salt and black pepperand beat until well combined.

11. Add arugula and tomatoes and toss to coat well.

12. Divide the salad onto on serving plates and top each with 1 patty.

13. Serve immediately.

Per serving:	Calories 329,	Fat 15.8g,	Carbs 24g,	Protein 24.9g,	Sodium 177mg

Chicken with Broccoli & Mushrooms

Preparation Time: **15 minutes**

Cooking Time: **25 minutes**

Servings: **6**

What you need:

- 3 tablespoons olive oil

- 1-pound skinless, boneless chicken breast, cubed

- 1 medium onion, chopped

- 6 garlic cloves, minced

- 2 cups fresh mushrooms, sliced

- 16 ounces small broccoli florets

- ¼ cup water

- Salt and ground black pepper, to taste

Method:

1. Heat the oil in a large wok over medium heat and cook the chicken cubes for about 4–5 minutes.

2. With a slotted spoon, transfer the chicken cubes onto a plate.

3. In the same wok, add the onion and sauté for about 4–5 minutes.

4. Add the mushrooms and cook for about 4–5 minutes.

5. Stir in the cooked chicken, broccoli and water and cook (covered) for about 8–10 minutes, stirring occasionally.

6. Stir in salt and black pepper and remove from heat.

7. Serve hot.

Per C 10. C 8. Pro 20. s 82

serv alorie 1 1g arbs 5 tei 1g, odium m

ing: s 97, at , g, n g

Lemon Ricotta Cookies with Lemon Glaze

Preparation Time: 10 Minutes

Cooking Time: **15 Minutes**

Servings: **10**

What you need:

- 2 ½ cups all-purpose flour

- 1 tsp. baking powder

- 1 tsp. salt

- 1 tbsp. unsalted butter softened

- 2 cups of sugar

- 2 eggs

- 1 teaspoon (15-ounces) container whole-milk ricotta cheese

- 3 tbsp. lemon juice

- zest of one lemon

Glaze:

- 11/2 cups powdered sugar

- 3 tbsp. lemon juice

- zest of one lemon

Method:

1. Preheat the oven to 375 degrees f.

2. Prepare a medium bowl; combine the flour, baking powder and salt. Set-aside.

3. From the big bowl, blend the butter and the sugar. With an electric mixer, beat the sugar and butter until light and fluffy, about three minutes. Then add eggs one at a time, beating until incorporated.

4. Insert the ricotta cheese, lemon juice and lemon zest. Beat to blend. Stir in the dry ingredients.

5. Line two baking sheets with parchment paper. Spoon the dough (approximately 2 tablespoons of each cookie) on the prepared baking sheets.

6. Then bake for 15 minutes or until slightly golden at the borders. Remove from the oven and allow the cookies to remain on the baking sheet for about 20 minutes.

7. For Glaze: combine the powdered sugar, lemon juice and lemon zest in a small bowl and then stir until smooth. Spoon approximately 1/2-tsp on each cookie and use of the back of the spoon to disperse lightly. Allow glaze to harden for approximately two hours. Pack the biscuits in a decorative jar.

Per serving:

- Calories: 360 Cal

- Fat: 2.5 g

- Carbs: 82.3 g

- Fiber: 0.9 g

- Protein: 4.5 g

Dark Chocolate Pretzel Cookies

Preparation Time: 20 Minutes

Cooking Time: **25 Minutes**

Servings: **4**

What you need:

- 1 cup yogurt
- 1/2 tsp. baking soda
- 1/4 teaspoon of salt
- 1/4 tsp. cinnamon
- 4 tbsp. butter (softened/0
- 1/3 cup brown sugar
- 1 egg
- 1/2 tsp. vanilla
- 1/2 cup dark chocolate chips
- 1/2 cup pretzels, chopped

Method:

1. Preheat the oven to 350 degrees.

2. First, whisk together the butter, sugar, vanilla and egg in a medium mixing bowl.

3. In a separate bowl, place and stir together the salt, baking soda and flour.

4. Stir the bread mixture in, using all the wet components, along with the chocolate chips and pretzels until just blended.

5. Drop a large spoonful of dough on a baking sheet (unlined).

6. Bake for 15-17 minutes, or until the bottoms are somewhat all crispy.

7. Allow cooling on a wire rack.

Per serving:

- Calories: 392 Cal

- Fat: 18.2 g

- Carbs: 50.2 g

- Fiber: 1 g

- Protein: 9.1 g

Mascarpone Cheesecake with Almond Crust

Preparation Time: 5 Minutes

Cooking Time: **10 Minutes**

Servings: **4**

What you need:

Crust:

- 1/2 cup slivered almonds

- 8 tsp. -- or 2/3 cup graham cracker crumbs

- 2 tbsp. sugar

- 1 tbsp. salted butter melted

Filling:

- 1 (8-ounces) packages cream cheese, room temperature

- 1 (8-ounces) container mascarpone cheese, room temperature

- 3/4 cup sugar

- 1 tsp. fresh lemon juice (I needed to use imitation lemon-juice)

- 1 tsp. vanilla extract

- 2 large eggs, room temperature

Method:

For the crust:

1. First, preheat oven to 350 degrees F. You will need a 9-inch pan (I had a throw off). Finely grind the almonds, cracker crumbs sugar in a food processor (I used my Magical Bullet). Then add the butter and process until moist crumbs form.

2. Press the almond mixture on the base of the prepared pan (maybe not on the edges of the pan). Bake the crust until its set and start to brown, about 1-2 minutes. Cool. Reduce the oven temperature to 325 degrees F.

3. For your filling: with an electric mixer, beat the cream cheese, mascarpone cheese and sugar in a large bowl until smooth, occasionally scraping down the sides of the jar using a rubber spatula. Beat in the lemon juice and vanilla. Add the eggs one at a time and beat until combined after each addition.

4. Pour the cheese mixture on the crust from the pan. Put the pan into a big skillet or Pyrex dish pour enough hot water to the roasting pan to come halfway up the sides of one's skillet. Bake until the middle of the filling moves slightly when the pan is gently shaken, about 1 hour (the dessert will get hard when it's cold). Transfer the cake to a stand; cool for 1 hour. Refrigerate until the cheesecake is cold, at least eight hours.

5. Topping: squeeze just a small thick cream in the microwave using a chopped Lindt dark chocolate - afterward, get a Ziplock baggie and cut out a hole at the

corner, then pour the melted chocolate into the baggie and used this to decorate the cake!

Per serving:

- Calories: 550 Cal
- Fat: 40.7 g
- Carbs: 36.9 g
- Fiber: 3.5 g
- Protein: 11.5 g

Home-made Ice Cream Drumsticks

Preparation Time: 20 Minutes

Cooking Time: **0 Minutes**

Servings: **4**

What you need:

- Vanilla ice cream
- Two Lindt hazelnut chunks
- Magical shell - out chocolate
- Sugar levels
- Nuts (I mixed crushed peppers and unsalted peanuts)
- Parchment paper

Method:

1. Soften ice cream and mixing topping - I had two sliced Lindt hazelnut balls.

2. Fill underside of Magic shell with sugar and nuts and top with ice-cream.

3. Wrap parchment paper round cone and then fill cone over about 1.5 inches across the cap of the cone (the paper can help to carry its shape).

4. Sprinkle with magical nuts and shells.

5. Freeze for about 20 minutes before the ice cream is eaten.

Per serving:

- Calories: 419 Cal

- Fat: 18.6 g

- Carbs: 63.6 g

- Fiber: 2.9 g

- Protein: 5 g

Peach and Blueberry Pie

Preparation Time: 10 Minutes

Cooking Time: **40 Minutes**

Servings: **16**

What you need:

- 1 box of noodle dough

Filling:

- 5 peaches, peeled and chopped (I used roasted peaches)

- 3 cups strawberries

- 3/4 cup sugar

- 1/4 cup bread

- Juice of 1/2 lemon

- 1 egg yolk, beaten

Method:

1.   Preheat oven to 400 degrees.

2.   Place dough to a 9-inch pie plate

3.   In a big bowl, combine tomatoes, sugar, bread and lemon juice, then toss to combine. Pour into the pie plate, mounding at the center.

4.   Simply take some bread and then cut into bits, then put a pie shirt and put the dough in addition to pressing on edges.

5.   Brush crust with egg wash then sprinkles with sugar.

6.   Set onto a parchment paper-lined baking sheet.

7.   Bake at 400 for about 20 minutes, until crust is browned at borders.

8.   Turn oven down to 350, bake for another 40 minutes.

9.   Remove and let sit at least 30 minutes.

10. Have with vanilla ice-cream.

Per serving:

- Calories: 80 Cal
- Fat: 1.1 g
- Carbs: 17.8 g
- Fiber: 1.3 g
- Protein: 1.1 g

Pear, Cranberry and Chocolate Crisp

Preparation Time: 15 Minutes

Cooking Time: **10 Minutes**

Servings: **10**

What you need:

- 1/2 cup flour

- 1/2 cup brown sugar

- 1 tsp. cinnamon

- 1/8 tsp. salt

- 3/4 cup yogurt

- 1/4 cup sliced peppers

- 1/3 cup butter, melted

- 1 teaspoon vanilla

Filling:

- 1 tbsp. brown sugar

- 1/4 cup dried cranberries

- 1 teaspoon of lemon juice

- Two handfuls of milk chocolate chips

Method:

1. Preheat oven to 375.

2. Spray a casserole dish with a butter spray.

3. Put all of the topping **ingredients** — flour, sugar, cinnamon, salt, nuts, etc.

4. Butter a bowl and then mix. Set aside.

5. In a large bowl, combine the sugar, lemon juice, pears and cranberries.

6. Once is fully blended, move to the prepared baking dish.

7. Spread the topping evenly over the fruit.

8. Bake for about half an hour.

9. Disperse chocolate chips out at the top.

10. Cook for another 10 minutes.

11. Have with ice cream.

Per serving:

- Calories: 128 Cal

- Fat: 6.6 g

- Carbs: 15 g

- Fiber: 0.7 g

- Protein: 2 g

Crunchy Chocolate Chip Coconut Macadamia Nut Cookies

Preparation Time: 10 Minutes

Cooking Time: **10 Minutes**

Servings: **10**

What you need:

- 1 cup yogurt

- 1 cup yogurt

- 1/2 tsp. baking soda

- 1/2 tsp. salt

- 1 tbsp. of butter, softened

- 1 cup firmly packed brown sugar

- 1/2 cup sugar

- 1 large egg

- 1/2 cup semi-sweet chocolate chips

- 1/2 cup sweetened flaked coconut

- 1/2 cup coarsely chopped dry-roasted macadamia nuts

- 1/2 cup raisins

Method:

1. Preheat the oven to 325°f.

2. In a little bowl, whisk together the flour, oats and baking soda and salt, then place aside.

3. In your mixer bowl, mix the butter/sugar/egg mix.

4. Mix in the flour/oats mix until just combined and stir into the chocolate chips, raisins, nuts and coconut.

5. Place outsized bits on a parchment-lined cookie sheet.

6. Bake for 1-3 minutes before biscuits are only barely golden brown.

7. Remove from the oven and then leave the cookie sheets to cool at least 10 minutes.

Per serving:

- Calories: 243 Cal

- Fat: 12.6 g

- Carbs: 30.3 g

- Fiber: 1.5 g

- Protein: 4.4 g

Ultimate Chocolate Chip Cookie N' Oreo Fudge Brownie Bar

Preparation Time: 15 Minutes

Cooking Time: **60 Minutes**

Servings: **10**

What you need:

- 1 cup (2 sticks) butter, softened

- 1 cup granulated sugar

- 3/4 cup light brown sugar

- 2 large eggs

- 1 tablespoon pure vanilla extract

- 2 ½ cups all-purpose flour

- 1 tsp. baking soda

- 1 tsp. lemon

- 2 cups (12 oz.) milk chocolate chips

- 1 package double-stuffed Oreo

- 1 family-size (9×1 3) brownie mixture

- 1/4 cup hot fudge topping

Method:

1. Preheat oven to 350 degrees F.

2. First, cream the butter and sugars in a bowl using an electric mixer at medium speed for 35 minutes.

3. Add the vanilla and eggs and mix well to combine thoroughly. In a separate bowl, whisk together the salt, flour and baking soda then slowly incorporate it in the mixer until everything is combined.

4. Stir in chocolate chips.

5. Spread the cookie dough at the bottom of a 9×1-3 baking dish that is wrapped with wax paper and then coated with cooking spray.

6. Shirt with a coating of Oreos. Mix brownie mix, adding an optional 1/4 cup of hot fudge directly into the mixture.

7. Stir the brownie batter within the cookie-dough and Oreos.

8. Cover with a foil and bake it at 350 degrees F for 30 minutes.

9. Remove foil and continue baking for another 15 25 minutes.

10. Let cool before cutting on brownies. They may be gooey while warm but will also set up perfectly once chilled.

Per serving:

- Calories: 490 Cal

- Fat: 21.9 g
- Carbs: 69 g
- Fiber: 1.5 g
- Protein: 5.5 g

Radish green pesto

Preparation Time: 15 Minutes

Cooking Time: **60 Minutes**

Servings: **10**

What you need:

- 2 handfuls

- fresh radish leaf (from 1–2 bunch of radishes in organic quality)

- 1 garlic

- 30 g pine nuts (2 tbsp)

- 30 g parmesan (1 piece; 30% fat in dry matter)

- 100 ml olive oil

- salt

- pepper

- 1 tsp lemon juice

Method:

1. Wash the radish leaves and shake them dry. Peel and chop the garlic.

2. Roast pine nuts in a hot pan without fat over medium heat for 3 minutes. Grate the Parmesan finely.

3. Puree the radish leaves, garlic, pine nuts and the oil with a hand blender. Mix in the Parmesan. Season with salt, pepper and lemon juice.

Watercress smoothie

Preparation Time: 15 Minutes

Cooking Time: **60 Minutes**

Servings: **10**

What you need:

- 150 g watercress
- 1 small onion
- ½ cucumber
- 1 tbsp lemon juice
- 200 ml mineral water
- salt
- pepper
- 4 tbsp crushed ice

Method:

1. Wash and spin dry watercress; put some sheets aside for the garnish.

2. Peel the onion and cut it into small cubes. Wash the cucumber half, halve lengthways and cut the pulp into tiny cubes; Set aside 4 tablespoons of cucumber cubes.

3. Puree the remaining cucumber cubes with cress, onion cubes, lemon juice, mineral water and ice in a blender.

4. Season the smoothie with salt and pepper, pour into 2 glasses and sprinkle with cucumber cubes and cress leaves.

Melon and spinach juice with cinnamon

Preparation Time: 15 Minutes

Cooking Time: **60 Minutes**

Servings: **10**

What you need:

- 350 g small honeydew melon (0.5 small honeydew melons)

- 250 g young tender spinach leaves

- 1 PC cinnamon stick (approx. 1 cm)

- nutmeg

Method:

1. Core the melon with a teaspoon. First cut the melon into wedges, then cut the pulp from the skin and roughly dice.

2. Clean the spinach and wash thoroughly in a bowl of water. Renew the water several times until it remains clear.

3. Using a small sharp knife, scrape thin strips off the cinnamon stick.

4. Squeeze the spinach lightly; Put back a leaflet and a small stem for the garnish as you like. Juice the rest with the melon in a juicer and pour it into a glass with ice

cubes. Rub a little nutmeg over it, garnish with cinnamon and possibly with the spinach set aside and enjoy immediately.

Christmas cocktail - vegan eggnog

Ingredients

- 1 cup cashew nuts
- 1 cup soy or almond milk
- 2-3 glasses of water
- about 5 pieces of dates (more if you like sweeter drinks)
- 2-3 scoops of brandy or whiskey
- 1 tablespoon lemon juice (optional, to taste)
- 1-2 teaspoons cinnamon
- ½ teaspoons ground anise
- ½ teaspoons ground ginger
- 2 pinches nutmeg
- pinch of salt

Method:

1. Pour dates and cashews with boiling water and leave to soak for 20 minutes. Transfer the remaining ingredients to the blender dish and finally add the drained nuts and dates.

2. Mix thoroughly in a high-speed blender for a few minutes, until a thick and creamy cocktail without lumps is formed. If your blender can't do it, mix the cashews with water first and strain them with gauze.

3. Season the cocktail with more lemon juice and salt to tasteand if you prefer sweeter drinks, add 2-3 pieces of dates. Serve it chilled with a pinch of cinnamon.

Orange and mandarin liqueur

Preparation Time: 15 Minutes

Cooking Time: **60 Minutes**

Servings: **10**

What you need:

- 2 large oranges
- 2 tangerines
- 1 small lemon
- 300 g white sugar candy
- 1 stick of vanilla
- 50 ml of orange juice
- 250 ml double grain

Method:

1. Put the sugar candy in a bottle or a screw-top jar.
2. Pour the citrus into small pieces and remove the skin.
3. Pour in the orange juice.
4. Add the vanilla stick.
5. Baste with the double grain
6. Fill up to the top of the bottle if desired.
7. Close the bottle.

8. Shake daily until the sugar candy has dissolved.

9. After 2 - 3 weeks pour the liqueur through a sieve.

10. Pour it back into the bottle.

Cucumber-apple-banana shake

Preparation Time: 15 Minutes

Cooking Time: **60 Minutes**

Servings: **10**

What you need:

- 1 lemon

- 1 banana

- 4th sour apples (e.g. granny smith)

- 1 bunch parsley

- ½ cucumber

- mineral water to fill up

- 10 dice ice cubes

Method:

1. Halve the lemon and squeeze out the juice. Peel and dice the banana. Clean, wash, quarter the apples, remove the core, dice the pulp. Mix the apples with the banana cubes and lemon juice.

2. Wash parsley, shake dry and chop. Clean, peel and halve the cucumber, coreand cut into bite-size pieces. Put 3 pieces of cucumber on 4 wooden skewers.

3. Puree the remaining pieces of cucumber with fruit, parsley and ice in a blender. Spread over 4 glasses, fill up with mineral water to the desired consistency and garnish with 1 cucumber skewer each.

Kefir avocado shake with herbs

Preparation Time: 15 Minutes

Cooking Time: **60 Minutes**

Servings: **10**

What you need:

- 2 stems dill
- 2 stems parsley
- straws of chives
- 1 avocado
- 1 tsp honey
- 1 splash lime juice
- 4 ice cubes
- 300 ml kefir chilled
- salt
- 1 pinch wasabi powder

Method:

1. Spray the herbs, pat dry, pluck and cut roughly except for a few dill tips for the garnish.

2. Peel, halve, core and cut the avocado into pieces. Puree with the herbs, honey, lime juice, ice cubes and kefir in a blender until creamy.

3. Season the smoothie with salt and wasabi and pour into glasses. Serve garnished with dill tips.

Mandarin liqueur

Preparation Time: 15 Minutes

Cooking Time: **60 Minutes**

Servings: **10**

What you need:

- 2 large oranges

- 2 tangerines

- 1 small lemon

- 300 g white sugar candy

- 1 stick of vanilla

- 50 ml of orange juice

- 250 ml double grain

Method:

1. Put the sugar candy in a bottle or a screw-top jar.

2. Pour the citrus into small pieces and remove the skin.

3. Pour in the orange juice.

4. Add the vanilla stick.

5. Baste with the double grain and fill up to the top of the bottle if desired.

6. Close the bottle.

7. Shake daily until the sugar candy has dissolved.

8. After 2 - 3 weeks pour the liqueur through a sieve and pour it back into the bottle.

• Pear and lime marmalade

Ingredients for 1.5 l jam

- 3-4 untreated limes

- 1 kg ripe pears

- 500 g jam sugar 2: 1

Method:

1. Wash 2 limes and grate dry.

2. Peel the peels thinly with the zest ripper.

3. Then cut all limes in half and squeeze them out. Measure out 100 ml of lime juice.

4. Wash and peel the pears, remove the core and then quarter them. Weigh 900 g of pulp.

5. Then puree the pears together with the lime juice.

6. Now put the pear puree together with the lime peels and the jellied sugar in a saucepan.

7. Bring all **ingredients** to the boil together.

8. Simmer for 4 minutes, stirring, taking care not to burn anything.

9. Make a gelation test with a small blob on a cold saucer. If this becomes solid in a short time, the jam is ready.

10. Remove any foam that may have formed with a spade, but you can also simply stir it in.

11. Then pour the hot mass into hot rinsed jars, close and let stand upside down.

Healthy green shot

Preparation Time: 15 Minutes

Cooking Time: **60 Minutes**

Servings: **10**

What you need:

- 2 pears
- 3 green apples (e.g. granny smith)
- 3 sticks celery
- 60 g organic ginger
- 1 bunch parsley (20 g)
- 3 kiwi fruit
- 2 limes
- 1 tsp turmeric

Method:

1. Wash pears, apples, celery, ginger and parsley and cut into pieces. Halve the kiwi fruit and remove the pulp with a spoon. Halve limes and squeeze out juice.

2. Put the pears, apples, kiwi, celery, ginger and parsley in the juicer and squeeze out the juice.

3. Mix freshly squeezed juice with the lime juice and season with turmeric. Serve the mixture as shots immediately or freeze it in portions.

Spinach kiwi smoothie bowl

Preparation Time: 15 Minutes

Cooking Time: **60 Minutes**

Servings: **10**

What you need:

- 1 green apple
- 2 kiwi fruit
- 300 g bananas (2 bananas)
- 100 g baby spinach
- 1 lemon
- 6 g chia seeds (2 tsp)
- 20 g grated coconut (2 tbsp)

Method:

1. Clean, wash, core and chop the apple. Peel and cut the kiwis and bananas and put half aside. Wash the spinach and put some leaves aside. Halve the lemon and squeeze out the juice.

2. Put half of the fruit, spinach and lemon juice in a blender and mash finely. Divide the smoothie into 4 bowls.

3. Put the remaining pieces of fruit as a topping on the smoothie bowls. Sprinkle with chia seeds and grated coconut and serve with the remaining spinach leaves.

Avocado smoothie with basil

Preparation Time: 15 Minutes

Cooking Time: **60 Minutes**

Servings: **10**

What you need:

- 2 kiwi fruit

- 1 yellow-peeled apple

- 200 g honeydew melon meat

- 1 avocado

- 1 green chili pepper

- 20 g basil (1 handful)

- 20 g arugula (0.25 bunch)

- 1 tbsp sprouts (suitable for raw consumption)

Method:

1. Peel and slice the kiwi fruit. Wash, quarter and core the apple and cut the quarters into slices. Cut the melon meat into pieces. Peel, core and cut avocado into pieces. Wash the chili pepper and cut it into rings. Wash the basil and rocket and shake dry. Shower sprouts in a sieve.

2. Put all prepared **ingredients** in a blender and mash them finely. Add about 100 ml of cold water and serve in 4 glasses.

Gooseberry buttermilk drink

Preparation Time: 15 Minutes

Cooking Time: **60 Minutes**

Servings: **10**

What you need:

- 300 g gooseberries

- 2 bananas

- 600 ml buttermilk

- 30 g honey (2 tbsp)

- 4 small stems of mint

- ice cubes

Method:

1. Wash and clean gooseberries and drain well. Set some berries aside for the garnish.

2. Peel and slice bananas. Puree together with gooseberries and 200 ml buttermilk. Add the remaining buttermilk and honey and mix until frothy.

3. Fill 4 glasses about halfway with ice cubes and spread the drink on them.

4. Wash the mint, shake it dry and spread it with the rest of the gooseberries on the drinks.

Blackberry and vanilla smoothie

Preparation Time: 15 Minutes

Cooking Time: **60 Minutes**

Servings: **10**

What you need:

- 500 g blackberry
- 1 vanilla bean
- 1 tsp lemon juice
- 700 ml buttermilk (ice cold)
- 80 g lean quark (4 tbsp)
- 40 g cashews
- 80 ml whipped cream

Method:

1. Wash and drain blackberries.
2. Cut the vanilla pod lengthways, scrape out the pulp and puree creamy with blackberries, lemon juice, buttermilk, curd cheese and cashew nuts in a blender.
3. Whip the cream. Pour smoothie into 4 glasses and garnish with cream

Dijon Celery Salad

Preparation Time: **10 minutes**

Cooking Time: **0 minutes**

Servings: **4**

What you need:

- 5 teaspoons stevia
- ½ cup lemon juice
- 1/3 cup dijon mustard
- 2/3 cup olive oil
- black pepper to the taste
- 2 apples, cored, peeled and cubed
- 1 bunch celery and leaves, roughly chopped
- ¾ cup walnuts, chopped

Method:

1. In a salad bowl, mix celery and its leaves with apple pieces and walnuts.
2. Add black pepper, lemon juice, mustard, stevia and olive oil.
3. Whisk well, add to your salad, toss.
4. Divide into small cups and serve as a snack.

Per serving:

Calories: 125 Cal

Fat: 2 g

Carbohydrates: 7 g

Protein: 7 g

Fiber: 2 g

Dill Bell Pepper Snack Bowls

Preparation Time: 10 minutes

Cooking Time: **0 minutes**

Servings: **4**

What you need:

- 2 tablespoons dill, chopped

- 1 yellow onion, chopped

- 1-pound multicolored bell peppers, cut into halves, seeded and cut into thin strips

- 3 tablespoons olive oil

- 2 and ½ tablespoons white vinegar

- Black pepper to the taste

Method:

1. In a salad bowl, mix bell peppers with onion, dill, pepper, oil and vinegar, toss to coat, divide into small bowls and serve as a snack.

Per serving:

Calories: 120 Cal

Fat: 3 g

Carbohydrates: 2 g

Protein: 3 g

Fiber: 3 g

Cinnamon Apple Chips

Preparation Time: **10 minutes**

Cooking Time: **2 hours**

Servings: 4

What you need:

Cooking spray

2 teaspoons cinnamon powder

2 apples, cored and thinly sliced

Method:

Arrange apple slices on a lined baking sheet, spray them with cooking oil, sprinkle cinnamon, introduce in the oven and bake at 300 degrees F for 2 hours.

Divide into bowls and serve as a snack.

Per serving:

Calories: 80 Cal

Fat: 0 g

Carbohydrates: 7 g

Protein: 4 g

Fiber: 3 g

Potato Bites

Preparation Time: **10 minutes**

Cooking Time: **20 minutes**

Servings: **3**

What you need:

1 potato, sliced

2 bacon slices, already cooked and crumbled

1 small avocado, pitted and cubed

Cooking spray

Method:

Spread potato slices on a lined baking sheet, spray with cooking oil, introduce in the oven at 350 degrees F, bake for 20 minutes, arrange on a platter, top each slice with avocado and crumbled bacon and serve as a snack.

Per serving:

Calories: 180 Cal

Fat: 4 g

Carbohydrates: 8 g

Protein: 6 g

Fiber: 1 g

Beans Snack Salad

Preparation Time: **10 minutes**

Cooking Time: **0 minutes**

Servings: **6**

What you need:

- 2 cups tomatoes, chopped

- 2 cups cucumber, chopped

- 3 cups mixed greens

- 2 cups mung beans, sprouted

- 2 cups clover sprouts

- for the salad dressing:

- 1 tablespoon cumin, ground

- 1 cup dill, chopped

- **4 tablespoons lemon juice**

- 1 avocado, pitted, peeled and roughly chopped

- 1 cucumber, roughly chopped

Method:

1. In a salad bowl.

2. Mix tomatoes with 2 cups cucumber, greens, clover and mung sprouts.

3. In your blender, mix cumin with dill, lemon juice, 1 cucumber and avocado.

4. Blend well, add this to your salad, toss well and serve as a snack.

Per serving:

Calories: 120 Cal

Fat: 0 g

Carbohydrates: 1 g

Protein: 6 g

Fiber: 2 g

Sprouts and Apple Snack Salad

Preparation Time: **10 minutes**

Cooking Time: **0 minute**

Servings: **4**

What you need:

- 1-pound brussels sprouts, shredded
- 1 cup walnuts, chopped
- 1 apple, cored and cubed
- 1 red onion, chopped
- For the salad dressing:
- 3 tablespoons red vinegar

- 1 tablespoon mustard

- *1/2* cup olive oil

- 1 garlic clove, minced

- Black pepper to the taste

Method:

1. In a salad bowl, mix sprouts with apple, onion and walnuts.

2. In another bowl, mix vinegar with mustard, oil, garlic and pepper, whisk well, add this to your salad, toss well and serve as a snack.

Per serving:

Calories: 120 Cal

Fat: 2 g

Carbohydrates: 8 g

Protein: 6 g

Fiber: 2 g

CPSIA information can be obtained
at www.ICGtesting.com
Printed in the USA
LVHW080459190721
693057LV00007B/380